Atmospheric Rivers: The Phenomenon Shaping Global Weather

Introduction:

Atmospheric rivers are a fascinating and impactful weather phenomenon that plays a significant role in the global climate system.

These narrow corridors of concentrated moisture in the atmosphere are responsible for transporting vast amounts of water vapor from the tropics to mid-latitudes, leading to significant precipitation events.

This book delves into the origins of atmospheric rivers, their effects across various regions, and their potential future implications in the context of climate change.

What Are Atmospheric Rivers?

Atmospheric rivers (ARs) are long, narrow bands of water vapor that extend from the tropics to higher latitudes.

They are typically 250-375 miles wide and can stretch for thousands of miles.

When these rivers of moisture make landfall, they can release large amounts of rain or snow, often causing extreme weather events such as floods and landslides.

Key Characteristics

- Width:

250-375 miles

- Length:

Up to several thousand miles

- Water Content:

Can transport 7.5-15 times the average flow of water at the mouth of the Mississippi River

<u>The Origins of Atmospheric Rivers</u>

Atmospheric rivers form when warm, moist air from the tropics is transported northward by strong winds.

The primary source of this moisture is the warm ocean waters near the equator.

As this moist air moves poleward, it is channeled into narrow bands by atmospheric conditions, including the presence of high and low-pressure systems.

Key Processes in Formation

- Evaporation:

Warm ocean waters near the equator evaporate, increasing the moisture content in the air.

- Convergence:

Moist air converges into narrow bands due to atmospheric circulation patterns.

- Transport:

Strong winds in the upper atmosphere transport these bands of moisture toward the mid-latitudes.

Global Impact of Atmospheric Rivers

Atmospheric rivers are a global phenomenon and have significant impacts on weather and climate in various regions around the world.

Their effects can be both beneficial and detrimental, depending on the intensity and duration of the event.

North America

In North America, atmospheric rivers are most commonly associated with the west coast of the United States and Canada.

The most well-known AR in this region is the "Pineapple Express," which brings moisture from the tropical Pacific near Hawaii to the West Coast.

- Benefits:

Provides much-needed rainfall to California and the Pacific Northwest, replenishing water supplies and supporting agriculture.

- Drawbacks:

Can cause severe flooding, landslides, and infrastructure damage. For example, the 1862 California Flood, also known as the Great Flood, was caused by a series of atmospheric rivers and led to widespread devastation.

Europe

Atmospheric rivers also impact Europe, particularly the United Kingdom and the Iberian Peninsula.

These regions can experience significant rainfall events when ARs make landfall.

- Benefits:

Contributes to water resources, especially during dry periods.

- Drawbacks:

Can lead to flooding and disruptions in transportation and infrastructure. The UK, for instance, experienced severe flooding in the winter of 2015-2016 due to atmospheric rivers.

South America

In South America, atmospheric rivers primarily affect the western coast, particularly Chile.

The phenomenon is known locally as "rivers in the sky" and can bring substantial rainfall to arid regions.

- Benefits:

Provides crucial rainfall to regions like the Atacama Desert, one of the driest places on Earth.
- Drawbacks:

Can cause flash floods and landslides, posing risks to communities and infrastructure.

Asia

Atmospheric rivers impact parts of Asia, including the Indian subcontinent and Southeast Asia.

They play a role in the monsoon systems that are vital for agriculture in these regions.

- Benefits:

Enhances monsoon rains, which are essential for crop irrigation and water supply.

- Drawbacks:

Intense rainfall can lead to flooding, landslides, and displacement of populations.

Effects on the Environment and Society

The impact of atmospheric rivers on the environment and society is profound.

While they are essential for delivering precipitation and replenishing water supplies, their extreme nature can also result in significant challenges.

Flooding and Landslides

One of the most immediate and visible impacts of atmospheric rivers is flooding.

When large amounts of moisture are released over a short period, rivers and streams can overflow, leading to widespread flooding.

This can have devastating effects on communities, infrastructure, and ecosystems.

- Case Study:

The 2019-2020 winter season in the Pacific Northwest saw several atmospheric river events that caused extensive flooding and landslides, disrupting communities and causing millions of dollars in damage.

Water Supply and Drought Mitigation

Atmospheric rivers are crucial for maintaining water supplies in many regions.

They provide much-needed precipitation during dry periods and help mitigate the effects of drought.

- Example:

California relies heavily on atmospheric rivers for its water supply. The state experiences a Mediterranean climate with wet winters and dry summers, making these moisture-laden systems vital for replenishing reservoirs and aquifers.

Agriculture and Food Security

The precipitation brought by atmospheric rivers supports agriculture, which is vital for food security.

Many agricultural regions depend on the seasonal influx of moisture to sustain crops.

- Impact:

In regions like the Central Valley of California, atmospheric rivers provide essential water for crops such as fruits, vegetables, and nuts.

 However, excessive rainfall can also damage crops and soil.

Infrastructure and Economic Impact

The economic impact of atmospheric rivers can be significant.

Flooding and landslides can damage infrastructure, disrupt transportation networks, and result in costly repairs and recovery efforts.

- Example:

The 2017 Oroville Dam crisis in California was exacerbated by intense rainfall from atmospheric rivers.

 The emergency spillway was damaged, leading to the evacuation of nearly 200,000 people and highlighting the vulnerability of infrastructure to extreme weather events.

The Future of Atmospheric Rivers in a Changing Climate

As the climate continues to change, the behavior and impact of atmospheric rivers are expected to evolve.

Climate models suggest that atmospheric rivers will become more intense and frequent, leading to a range of potential implications.

Increased Intensity and Frequency

Warmer global temperatures result in higher evaporation rates, increasing the moisture content in the atmosphere.

This can lead to more intense atmospheric rivers with greater potential for heavy precipitation and flooding.

- Projection:

Studies indicate that the frequency of strong atmospheric rivers could double by the end of the century, with the most significant increases expected in the North Pacific and North Atlantic regions.

Enhanced Flood Risks

With increased intensity, the risk of flooding from atmospheric rivers will likely rise.

Coastal and riverine communities will need to adapt to more frequent and severe flood events.

- Adaptation:

Improved forecasting, better infrastructure design, and enhanced emergency response plans will be critical in mitigating the risks associated with more intense atmospheric rivers.

Impact on Water Resources

While increased precipitation could benefit water resources in some regions, it may also lead to challenges in water management.

The timing and distribution of rainfall could become more erratic, complicating efforts to maintain reliable water supplies.

- Management Strategies:

Integrated water resource management approaches that account for the variability and extremes in precipitation will be essential in ensuring sustainable water supplies.

Ecological Implications

Changes in the frequency and intensity of atmospheric rivers can also have ecological implications.

Ecosystems that depend on seasonal rainfall patterns may be disrupted, affecting biodiversity and habitat stability.

- Example:

Forest ecosystems in the Pacific Northwest, which rely on consistent winter precipitation, may face stress from altered rainfall patterns, affecting tree health and increasing the risk of wildfires.

<u>Conclusion</u>

 Atmospheric rivers are a powerful and complex component of the Earth's climate system.

 They play a crucial role in transporting moisture and delivering precipitation to various regions, with significant implications for the environment, society, and economy.

As the climate continues to change, understanding and adapting to the evolving behavior of atmospheric rivers will be essential in managing their impacts and harnessing their benefits.

Through improved forecasting, infrastructure resilience, and adaptive water management, communities can better prepare for the challenges and opportunities presented by these remarkable weather phenomena.

Please use the next few pages for your notes and debates.